T0171634

Also available:

Piccadilly
By Larissa Houghton

Volume I of Intelligent Lessons
of Music Knowledge (Guitar and Piano)

INTELLIGENT LESSONS of MUSIC KNOWLEDGE (GUITAR AND PIANO) VOLUME II

Mary Sewall

iUniverse, Inc.
Bloomington

INTELLIGENT LESSONS of MUSIC KNOWLEDGE (GUITAR AND PIANO) VOLUME II

Copyright © 2010 by Mary Sewall

iUniverse books may be ordered through booksellers or by contacting:

iUniverse
1663 Liberty Drive
Bloomington, IN 47403
www.iuniverse.com
1-800-Authors (1-800-288-4677)

Because of the dynamic nature of the Internet, any Web addresses or links contained in this book may have changed since publication and may no longer be valid. The views expressed in this work are solely those of the author and do not necessarily reflect the views of the publisher, and the publisher hereby disclaims any responsibility for them.

ISBN: 978-1-4502-6280-4 (sc)
ISBN: 978-1-4502-6281-1 (ebook)

Printed in the United States of America

iUniverse rev. date: 3/10/2011

CONTENTS

```
*********************************
```

CHAPTER ONE

```
*****
```

LESSON 1

INTELLIGENT LESSONS OF MUSIC KNOWLEDGE
IS THE ABSENCE OF SOUND

(Guitar and Piano)

It is wonderful to be back with my darlings. Life being what it is one never knows what to expect from day to day, but here we are together again. I wonder what experience my musicians have had, since we left off from our first visit. I would love to hear about the up and down of the daily livings, especially in this troubling economy. People are losing their houses, and jobs.

The trials and tribulations are very real, and can bring much misery into our lives. This has always been part of life. When I think of Beethoven, one of the greatest musicians on this planet, with his soul pouring out his colossal music vibrating across the universe, to be in tune with this spiritualistic ethereal higher part of the mind, one could be at peace.

Ludwig van Beethoven, who was a German composer, had trouble paying his rent, so he had to move from place to place. Franz Peter Schubert, who was Austrian, had a great output of music, and was so poor his friends had to help feed him. Wolfgang Amadeus Mozart, Austrian, another giant in music, was so impoverished that when he died his body was thrown into a paupers grave.

I bring this up because they had a mission in life that just had to be fulfilled. Music is in every human being, of course in various degrees. With some it consumes their whole lives, and in others it just exist; it is part of our existence. It could lie dormant for a while, and then hit us at a later stage. So it is never too late to start.

The Greeks developed the highest civilization in the ancient world. Much of this has come to us. They handed down the alphabet (characters used for writing a language), which was acquired from the Phoenicians, and then passed to the Romans. The writing of music took centuries to reach us today.

The question is? How can it be absorbed in a few weeks? Most Guitars players in a rock band think so. They beat a few chords to death, and in the process do make millions of dollars. (Not Bad.) But can that be called professionalism. I think not. The same thing happens with the piano player in the group.

Aside from standing, and pounding the keys with the same amount of chords, while doing some gymnastics for theatrical effects, it certainly looks impressive. Further, the piano that is used is only a few octaves long. (Octave - means eight, the eight full tones above a given tone.) A standard piano has 88 keys, and of course is by far superior. So what--- one might say. Well, for one, many people don't notice the difference. A piano is a piano.

It is best to know about this. Some people never count the keys. The Guitar has only six strings. A beginner usually can't figure it out. Like, how can the two instruments be related, one, having 88 keys, and the other with only 6 strings. Well, this is for us to figure out

To clear this up, we need our alphabet that goes so far back in time. Yes, the same one that is used for our language. Many of you know the Alphabet Song: A-B-C-D-E-F-G---H-I-J-K-L-M-N-O-P---Q-R-S-T-U-V---W-X-Y-Z. Happy, happy, we shall be, when we learn our A-B-C's. ---26 letters of the alphabet.

The first 7 letters of this alphabet is all we use for our musical alphabet. It might seem so easy. Why? Because it has only 7 letters, but this is what fills our ocean of music.

TWINKLE, TWINKLE, LITTLE STAR
Verse
Generally a sentence, or part of a sentence
Twinkle, Twinkle, Little Star
How I wonder what you are
Up above the world so high
Like a diamond in the sky
Twinkle, Twinkle, Little star
How I wonder what you are
We now will look at the music version, and see how the Verse fits in.

TWINKLE, TWINKLE, LITTLE STAR

Look carefully at this version. There are 5 horizontal lines, which make 4 spaces. Then vertical lines that house black and white large dots with stems, some going up and others down in these boxes. They are called (notes) a tone of definite pitch. At the very beginning is a sign that looks like a curlicue, and then on the right of it a tic-tack-toe and lastly two, numbers, a 2 and 4. At the very end is a double line, which means the end of the piece. That about covers it Dears. Time to take a rest. ---

I hope everyone had a bit of time off. Now we'll wipe out the whole version, and look at a blank music manuscript paper. All we see are the 5 lines. Compare the contrast, and mentally study what went into those lines and spaces. Looking at the blank images, visualize and restore its order.

TREBLE CLEF

BLANK MANUSCRIPT PAPER

Mentally visualize what the original staff looked like (Staff, the five horizontal lines and the four spaces on which music is written). This could be therapeutic. It is easy on the eyes, as all we see is empty space. When you feel you are ready Darlings, depending what your state of mind and health is. Bring it back to your attention, and gently in your mind drop in the G Clef sign (a symbol used in music to indicate the pitch of the notes on the staff) Take notice of the curly cue that ends on the G note. It means that this G note will never change. It will always be written on the second line. From this we get all of our other notes, as this is the starting point.

If other things come to mind, let it run its course. Come back to the task at hand, and add the Sharp sign (raised in pitch by a semitone, or also called a half tone.) Now we turn our attention to the Key Signature (one or more sharps or flats, placed after the clef on the staff to indicate the key.) It means, instead of writing in the sharps or flats that is needed, it is placed at the beginning of the piece. That way it is played throughout the piece.

Time Signature (a sign after the Key Signature indicating the Time, or Tempo. It is amazing how little of this is taught at the music lesson, but even if it is, it does not seem to be comprehended. If this is done away from the instrument (whatever one it is) if it was gained in this manner, the mind will bring it back by remote control, because it was unhindered with too many attachments.

G-CLEF, SHARP, KEY SIGNATURE, TIME SIGNATURE, NOTES, BAR LINES, MEASURES

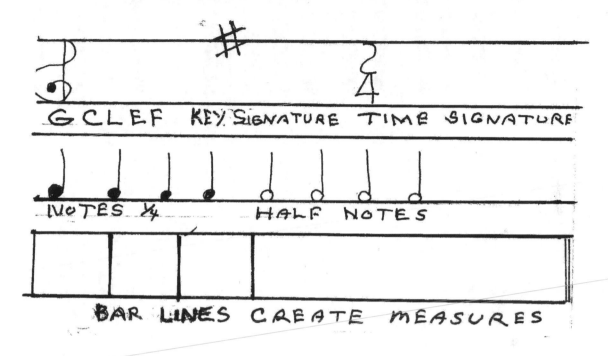

Now Dears we will tackle the Notes.

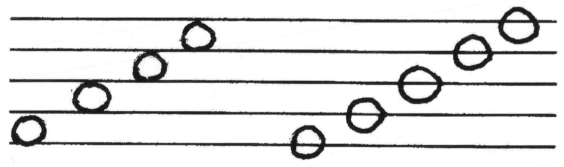

In the 1st Space is an F---2nd Space an A---3rd Space a C---4th Space E. It spells the word FACE. ---1st Line is an E---2nd Line a G---3rd Line B---4th Line D---5th Line F. It spells a Sentence. Every-Good-Boy-Does-Fine. Memorize this, as it will never change. It will forever be called that.

Turn to the song Twinkle, Twinkle, little Star, and Bingo! All the notes we just learned are in the song. All we have to do is carefully find them. The piano chart (Page 6) shows the black and white keys. Notice the two black and then three black keys. In between are the white--A-B-C-D-E-F-G---A-B-C-D-E-F-G. So, you see, once you learn where these 7 letters are from our musical alphabet, you are in good hands.

PIANO KEYBOARD

C D E F G A B C E G A B C

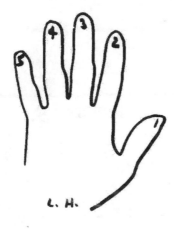 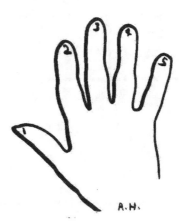

L. H.   R. H.

FINGERING

When playing a scale on the piano with the left hand (a scale consists of 8 tones.) put the whole hand on whatever scale you want to play. For this put your hand on the arm of a chair, or on your lap, as you wish. We use all of the fingers, thus. 5-4-3- 2- 1-. Now we have run out of fingers, Dears, so, we hang unto the thumb to make a smooth turnover, and swivel the 3rd finger, then let go of the thumb, and continue with the 2md finger- and finish with the thumb. Lets have a go with the right hand.

This is slightly different. Spread you right hand out. Play the thumb, then the 2nd, and next the 3rd. This time we hang unto the 3rd finger, and swivel the thumb under, until we get a smooth turnover, and once that is done, the rest of the finger finish the job, which is the 2nd, 3rd, 4th and lastly the 5th. It is fun when you really understand what is going on.

Trouble start when all of this is crushed together, and it is easy to understand why people walk away from it. When each step is mastered, we do want to continue.

COUNTING IS MATHEMATICAL

It seems strange that music is mathematical. But it surely is so. Rigorously exact, no ifs, and or buts about it. If the **Time Signature** says two-quarter time, it means exactly that. Two beats to a measure, and every quarter note gets one beat. This lasts throughout the whole piece. If the composer wants a different tempo he then changes it, but it is left up to the musician as the music is being created, but the pattern follow suit.

In our piece (Page 3) the 1st three measures are quarter notes. If we are on a bus, plane, train, or just sitting in our easy chair we could play this piece. Put your hand on the arm of the seat. Think of a ball. We slap the ball down, but once it comes up it has to be struck again to go down. This is done again and again to continue the process. Using this analogy is similar with our fingers. On the count of **ONE** the ball is struck, when it pops up we call it **AND --- ONE AND TWO AND.**

With the hand on the arm of the chair, fingers resting comfortably, Press the ball of the index finger until you feel the pressure (this is the soft tissue below the fingernail) we start thus-Pressure- Release- Pressure- Release. This is the bouncing ball-Down-Up-Down-Up, Darlings, I don't want to tax you strength, so another rest period. ---

The 4th measure is a half note. Press the finger down on the count of **ONE** and hold it for the two beats **ONE AND TWO AND**. On the last **AND** release the pressure. This process repeats itself for the remainder of the piece. There are 5 more repeats of the same 4 original measures, as far as the counting is concerned. This adds up to 6 complete sections. There are 24 measures in all.

The melody starts on the note G, and ends on the G. We are in the Key of G. This is known because the Key Signature has an F Sharp. Well Dears, where did this F Sharp come from. Everything has to be accounted for, so it had to come from somewhere. This now brings us the Dreaded Scales. Actually, the Scales hold the secret to it all. Most beginners run as fast as they can from them. The faster they run the less they learn. Once the Scales are unlocked, the mystery of music is opened up.

Down below is a sketch of a piano Octave.(Page 8, C to C) When we first learn our scales, we usually are given each new scale like they are foreign to each other. And each one seems to get more and more difficult, for the simple reason that as we climb the ladder from the 1st scale (which is C, going straight up without encountering any , difficulties we feel at ease with it.) When the next Scale is given; G, we hit an F#, and it certainly is different. This pattern goes on, until all the Scales are played, each one adding on one more sharp, or flat, and getting more and more difficult.

CHAPTER TWO

*****

LESSON 2

SCALES

When you look at this Scale, it seems to be so inviting. It is an Octave. Behind it lies the beginning of a world of music. Almost like a new mystery to be solved. It is true, because that is what it is. If you do not understand the theory of music, and you look at this scale it might not have much meaning to you. It is important to realize that music goes back centuries, so we must take this into account.

OCTAVE

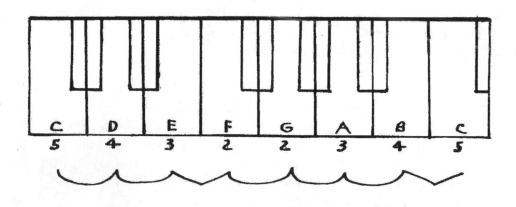

The Chart shows the **C SCALE**. It looks like a perfect scale because it has no black keys. But as we move along with the scales, they couldn't look more different. They are loaded with Sharps and Flats. The surprising thing is that all of the Major Keys are alike in their construction. I'm almost certain that if you studied piano many years ago, the scales were taught as having no connection to each other.

Each new scale that was added from week to week became more difficult to learn, and this process became more painful as we went along. Since they were taught that way, they were also memorized in this fashion. The added sharps and flats were encased in our memory bank. It most likely never entered our minds to view them any other way.

But Dears it is time to get to the truth of this matter.

ALL MAJOR SCALES ARE ALIKE IN THEIR CONSTRUCTION
THEY ARE EXACT REPRODUCTIONS OF EACH OTHER
THE ONLY DIFFERENCE IS THAT THEY VARY IN PITCH

APPRECIATING THE SCALES WILL OPEN MANY DOORS FOR US.

The Chart is divided into two sections. The left hand plays fingers 5-4-3-2-. Next the right hand plays 2-3-4-5-. We are leaving out the thumbs for this to create a Tetrachord. (Tetra meaning four-Tetrachord means four full tones, or otherwise half of an octave.) To learn the pattern for the scales, we will start with the left hand. Put your fingers on the chart, which is big enough to accommodate the fingers, Dears, if you need this help.

NOTICE

Place all the fingers on the chart, minus the thumb: 5-4-3-2---2-3-4-5. Between C and D is a whole step (meaning that there is a Key between). This is called a whole step. D-E is another whole step. Between E-F is a Half step. Now we take the right hand. This is separated by a whole step - Second finger plays F-still being the left hand, and second plays G, which is the right hand. This is what is meant by separated, and is a whole step. G-A is a whole step. A-B is a whole step. B-C is a half step. To understand this fully it is a good idea to actually place the fingers on the chart.

All of the major keys, sharps and flats have this same pattern. To find the next scale in order, count 5 from C, including the C---C-D-E-F-G. We now have the next scale, which happens to house our piece, and is in the Key of G. Now we will find out how we inherited the F#, but Darlings I think we need another break, including me. See you.

I'm back, and I hope you too had a bit of time off. I went downtown here on Market Street in Philadelphia, Pa. I love to go to the Food Court at the Mall. But I am always happy to return to my music. The G we left off with is our new scale. For this scale we use our pattern as we did for the C scale. Put the fingers of the tetrachord on the pattern. G-A is a whole step. A-B is a whole step. B-C is a half step. C-left hand- to D-right hand is called the separation, is a whole step. Continue--- D-E is a whole step. And E-F should be a whole step, but Dears we have fallen short. It is only a half step. What to do??? Our pattern tells us to raise the F to an F#, as we must have a whole, lastly we finish with the F# to G and we have our half step. So we really needed that break we took. The pattern gave us opportunity to raise the F to a sharp.

TIME FOR A NEW PIECE

For this piece we are going to the Key of C. No sharps or flats. The reason I started in the Key of G for the first one, was because all of the notes we used in the song were contained in the 5 lines and 4 four spaces. In this piece it holds the same concept, except we introduce a new note called G. After we run out of lines and spaces we must add new ones. Below I have some music manuscript paper. This will help explain how it is done. It does require some extra mental effort, so Dears be prepared for it.

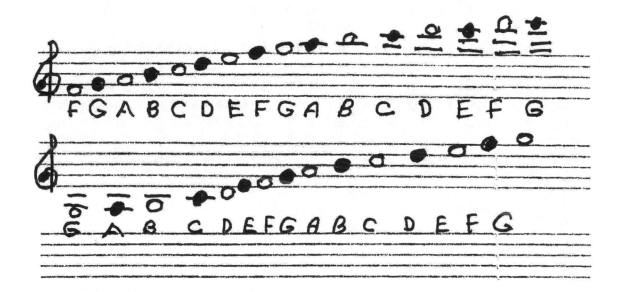

HIGH G NOTE

The new note G goes up the music alphabet in order. A-B-C-D-E-F- and G, We come across line and space notes. It is interesting to observe that since we are working with only 7 different letters, the written line and space notes do change. We could introduce some lower notes, but for now this could wait, unless you want to go backwards. You can go either way, up the hill, or down the hill. Going up is easy, just say the alphabet: G-A-B-C-D-E-F-G-A-B-C-D-E-F-G. Down the hill is more difficult. G-F-E-D-C-B-A-G-F-E-D-C-B-A-G. For now we are only interested in the new note G for our new piece.

WABASH CANNON BALL

The Key Signature is in C. Time Signature is 4-4 Time. There are four beats to a measure, and every quarter note gets one beat. Notice the first measure in incomplete, it starts out with two eighth notes. It takes two eighth notes to make a quarter note. However, if you look at the end of the piece, you will find the missing beats. This one has a dotted half note, two quarter notes make a half note. In a way it is like counting money. Two half notes are like two fifty-cent pieces and make a whole dollar or a whole note.

Now we play the piece, Darlings. Rest your hand on a Sofa, Chair, Bed, Bus Seat, Plane Seat, Hospital Bed, as a matter of fact, just about anywhere. Or if that is not available at the moment, squeeze your toes, then relax them, click your tongue up to the roof of the mouth and then let it drop down. We are really in earnest with this, and all fired up so lets charge ahead Dears.

For the first incomplete measure we count silently (meaning do not play anything, just count) 1 AND--2 AND--3 AND, then on the count of 4 we play the index finger, but on the count of AND we actually play the AND. So there you have it. Next measure is really the first full measure so we call it measure One; it has 4 quarter notes. We continue, bring the index finger down on the 1, but on the count of AND, we bring it up silently, and continue the same. 2 AND 3 AND 4 AND.

Measure Two, first beat is 1 AND, remember to bring the AND up silently. On the count of 2 (being a half note it must be held for two counts) we bring the finger down on the count of 2- hold it for the AND- plus the count of 3- bring it up on the AND. Finish it with the last two eighth notes. Which is counted as finger down on 4 plus the AND is played (be aware of the eighth notes).

Measure FOUR has a dotted half note. Bring the finger down on the count of 1 hold it for 1 AND 2 AND also 3 then bring it up on the AND. Finish it with the count of 4 by playing finger down on 4 this time you play the AND. The dot means that the measure before it is equal to half of the value. So half of the half note is a quarter note, (like counting money) and would get one beat. If the dot were to materialize it would look like a quarter note. Not to worry Dears if it appears foggy, it will clear up in due time.

Measure Seven has a dotted quarter note on the 3rd beat. Begin with the 1st beat. Play the index finger down on the 1 AND, but bring the AND up silently as before, continue with the 2nd but on the 3rd, being it has a dotted quarter note, play 3 but hold the AND, come up on the count of 4, then play the AND. (The dotted quarter note is equal to half of what is before it, which is a eighth note, half of a quarter is an eighth.)

Measure 12 is very easy. It is a whole note, we hold it for the full 4 counts, thus, on the count of 1 we play the index finger, count 1 AND 2 AND 3 AND 4 AND. Don't forget hold the whole 4 counts down. Just make sure you count it.

Measure 16, the last one has an incomplete measure. It has only three beats. You will find the missing 4th beat at the beginning of the piece. The reason this could happen is because the composer, when creating the piece wants to put the word Great on the 1st strong beat, and leaves the "from" on the weak beat. So Darlings, I hope I didn't stress you out too much, but the reward comes later on when you find all that we learned in a zillion other pieces.

A good idea is to look at some music and see how many pieces you could find that have the same features we covered in our piece. It is well worth the time to do this. When you get bored with the T.V. this will wake you up. The problem with the Television is that our brain is dulled with nothing to do but stare at the tube, and this in turn lulls us in a stupor, and we black out. When we do something constructive the brain comes to attention and comes to life again. When you want to get drowsy, turn the tube on again.

We will be going to the Guitar, and apply what we have learned from the Piano to this 6 string guitar. Many people have difficulty understanding how these two different instruments could possibility be related. Firstly the piano has 88 keys, and the guitar has only 6 strings

The piano keys are all laid out for the world to see. The guitar having only the 6 strings are certainly not easily comprehended, so dears we will travel along this journey and uncover the secret. Before we do I want to make clear the G Scale.

G SCALE CHART

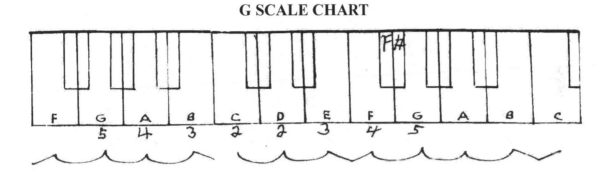

NOTE VALUES

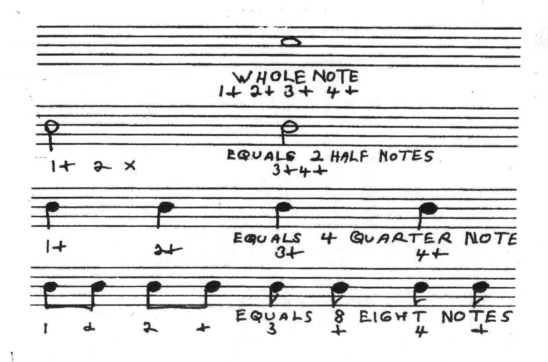

CHAPTER THREE

*****

LESSON 3

THE GUITAR

The Guitar is one of the most popular instruments. It is not only used to accompany soloists and vocal groups, but also as a band and solo instruments. A guitar has six strings, which are tuned in fourths, except for one irregular third in the upper register. The fingerboard has FRETS (narrow metal strips) against which the guitarist presses the strings with the fingers of his left hand.

The Guitarist strums or plucks the strings with his right hand, and may use a pick made of metal, plastic, or some other material. Guitars are made of light wood and have arched or flat tops and backs.

Electric Guitars produce louder and clearer tones than do non-electric models. A small microphone under the strings picks up the sound, which is sent through a loudspeaker. Since the early 1930's, Electric Guitars have become increasingly important in both popular and classical music.

Historians believe the Guitar was developed in the Middle East, around the time 1000 B.C. A piece of sculpture shows an instrument with some features of the Guitar. Of course the instrument has changed greatly since then, and continues to change as time goes by. Andres Segovia has used it to play beautiful classical music.

On page 15 we have the Guitar and the hand fingering, plus a picture of some CHORD DIAGRAMS on which chords are written. We could also play the melody. In classical music, which is very difficult to play, takes years and years of training. This is because the musician must read music. Aside from using the left hand to form the chords, the right hand does the melody, using all the fingers, including the thumb.

The Guitar

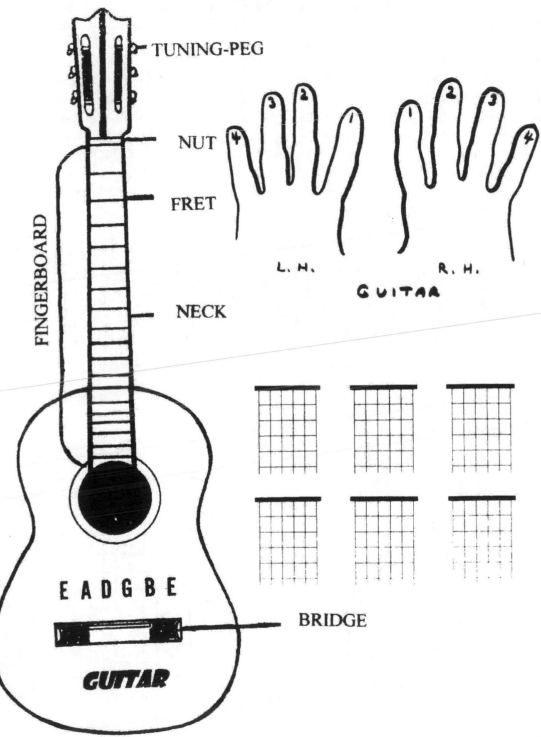

We will assume that the Guitar is in Tune. This could be done in a number of ways. When you went to Grade School Darlings, the music teacher would use a Pitch Pipe for the pupils to be in tune. If you happen to have a piano this could be another way to tune it. Below is a chart to show how it could be done.

The Piano Chart starts with the low E, the 6th string and lowest string on the Guitar. Count 4 up from this E, and the 5th string A pops up. Count 4 from A (including A) and we get the 4th string D. Count 4 from D and the 3rd string G comes up. Now be careful because we only count 3 from this G, and we get B. We are now back to normal. Count 4 from B and E comes up. To get the proper tune up with the Guitar on the Piano, we must find MIDDLE C. This occurs in the middle of the Piano, where the name of the instrument is stamped, and also happens to be in the middle of the Piano.

TUNE GUITAR

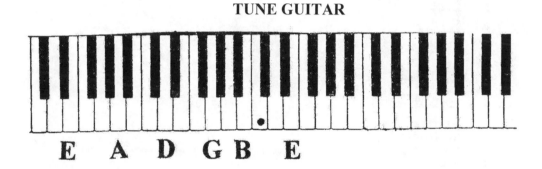

E   A   D   G   B   E

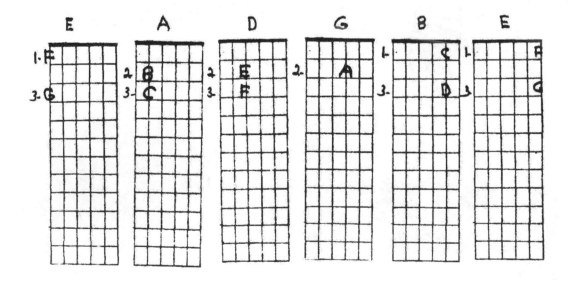

When and if you ever decide to buy a Guitar, the most important thing to look for is to make sure the strings are close to the Frets. In other words being unaware of this point, the cheap ones are usually too high from the frets, and you could end up playing on a board spring. Another thing do not buy one with the steel strings, as a beginners fingers will start to bleed, because they are very sensitive and must harden with time. Buy NYLON STRINGS or similar material.

With the Guitar cradled in your arms, rest your left foot on a short stool for comfort. Since we are learning without the instrument, picture it in your mind in this position. Put the left hand on the neck of the Guitar, and squeeze the index finger and the thumb to make a connection. Do the same with the 2nd 3rd and 4th fingers.

We will now add the right hand. Mentally rest the thumb of the R. hand (keep in mind the Guitar picture) on the low 6th string (over the sounding board where the round opening is). When the thumb is played, it is thrust away from the body, and lands on the 5th string, where it rests. Thrust the thumb from this string and it lands on the 4th string.

Start again and play the thumb on the 6th string. Darlings, what to do with the rest of the four fingers? Usually the hand is curved (this is a natural position at all times), so Dears we open the four finger and sweep them across the rest of the strings. Like the bouncing ball the hand must come back to the position to brush it away again, back to position and brushed away again. Instead of the hand brushing the strings, we could cut out a triangle from a plastic milk container. This is a homemade pick. Hold it between the thumb and index finger, and thrust it away as we did with the hand, and the wrist will fly with it.

Look at the 6 diagrams below the Piano Chart. Each one represents a Guitar String. Play the low E OPEN (meaning that the left hand does not participate in this exercise). Play in your mind the low E string with the thumb, remember to rest it on the next string. It should actually touch it, and really rest. Take a breather, and then continue this process with the rest of the strings, and really say each string as you play them.

I do hope Dears that you take time off as we go along. This could go a long way as these bits and pieces add up. I have my special little corner in my living room, with an easy chair and the end table to keep my papers. I try to keep it neat though. I like to be where all the action is, near the front door so I could see what is going on outside.

Now we add the left hand to the right hand. Starting again with the low E. Bring the naturally curved hand (with the palm facing you) over all the way to the 6th string and place the 1st finger on the 1st Fret. Do you notice how the wrist cooperates with this move? Now press this finger down and at the same time the thumb being much stronger will help support this movement. After all this work we are rewarded with a new note F. While holding the note play the 6th string with the right hand thumb. Take a rest and absorb what we have done. Then since we are on a roll, do the same thing with the 3rd finger, but on the 3rd Fret of the 6th string, and another note appears, G.

For now we are finished with the 6th string. Next we tackle the 5th string A Bring the 2nd finger and place it on the 2nd FRET of the 5th string and we get the note B. While holding it down play this B with the right-hand thumb on the 5th string. On the same string continue with the 3rd finger on the 3rd FRET and the note C appears, and play the right thumb on the same string.

The 4th string is D. We repeat what we just covered on the previous string, but the notes change to E and F. We move onto the 3rd string, which is G. We have only one note on the 2nd FRET and, played with the 2nd finger, called A. But instead of using the thumb of the right hand we will use the 1st finger of the right hand and play this A with a motion pulling the string toward your body, and resting on the string next to it.

On the 2nd string is a B. We put the 1st finger of the left hand onto the 1st FRET of this 2nd string, and we get a C, and play the right hand with the 2nd finger on the same string. Put the 3rd finger onto the 3rd FRET and we have a D, and play the right hand with the 2nd finger. Finally, we come to the high E string on the 1st string, and put the 1st finger on the 1st FRET and we get F, and play the right hand with the 3rd finger. And end up with the 3rd finger of the 3rd FRET G, and play the right hand with the 3rd finger. Notice that the low E and the high E are identical

WOW, that was quite a drill, Dears. Drop everything and make supper. That is what I am going to do after all that work. Well, Darlings I had my supper and now this is another day, so back to work after being refreshed. So where were we? Oh, I'm only kidding. Music has always been in my life.

When I was a child before I studied music, and being in Grade School, the teacher in charge had us all lined up for some reason, and as we passed there was a Piano, I put my hand down and I accidentally hit a key that had a profound effect on me and that started the whole thing. After that I would dream about Pianos.

CHORDS

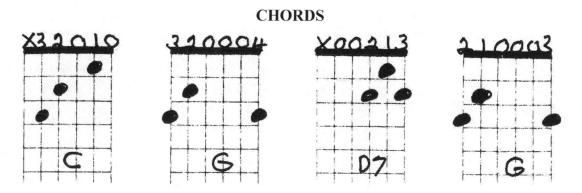

18

When playing Chords with the left hand, the thumb is used to wrap around the neck of the instrument. It takes time for this because the fingers are not accustomed to it. When we try it the fingers seems very weak. To strengthen them we must remember that the thumb has a big role in this. For instance, it is just impossible to catch a ball without using the thumb. It also applies to the guitar.

Sitting in your easy chair take the left hand and push all four finger toward you. Nothing really happens until the thumb is brought into play. This time push the thumb away from you at the same time as it hits the fingers, and apply pressure. The power is amazing. This is applied to the neck of the guitar. Darlings, don't laugh, because you might think, if you are bedridden, don't waste my time, but who knows, when you are up and about you just might get interested.

Now that we have the force, we could plunge forward. Looking at the chord Diagrams we see 6 lines which represent the strings of the instrument. We have two versions of the G Chord. They are the same, but for the fingering (You have a choice). We also have the C and D7 Chords: Only three Chords for our song. Study them in your spare time, if you want the time to fly by. Being absorbed in this manner takes your mind off unpleasant thoughts, and even agreeable ones.

For the C Chord the first string is open, so the left hand does nothing Dears. The 2nd string we put the 1st finger on the first fret, gives us the note C. The 3rd gives us an open string G. The 4th is played with the 2nd finger 2nd fret and is an E. The 5th string is played with the 3rd finger and is a C. The X on the low E, of the 6th string means do not play. In your mind play the chords and strung at the same time.

Usually when you buy Guitar Books these Chords just have the names of the Chords, as I have on page 18. Rarely are the actual letter names of each DOT exposed. So Dears we will have to go through them to understand them. Both of the G Chords are the same, except for the fingering. The first one has the fourth finger on the 3rd fret called G. The next three are open strings. The letters names are open B, G and D. The fifth string second finger, 2nd fret is B. The sixth with the third finger on the 3rd fret is G.

The last one is a D7 Chord. The first string, played with the 3rd finger 2nd fret, is F#. Second string is a C with the first finger. The third string with the 2nd finger is A. The fourth and fifth strings are open. The last E string is not played. When you are able, visit the Library's Music Department. There are many Folk Songs written with these three Chords for the Guitar. It is interesting to search them out, and pour over them.

Dears we won't go over the other Chords with such a minute microscope as it could get very tedious. In due time you will be able to figure it out for yourself. In the song for the Guitar Version of "Twinkle, Twinkle, Little Star" we have all three of the Chords we have studied. The added song "The Alphabet Song" has the same music as Twinkle, the only difference are the words.

TWINKLE, TWINKLE, LITTLE STAR

2/4

G | G | C | G | C | G |
TWIN-KLE | TWIN-KLE | LIT-TLE | STAR | HOW I | WON-DER

D7 | G | G | D7 | G | D7 |
WHAT YOU | ARE | UP A- | BOVE THE | WORLD SO | HIGH.

LIKE A

G | D7 | G | D7 | G | G |
LIKE A | DIA-MOND | IN THE | SKY | TWIN-KLE | TWIN-KLE

C | G | C | G | D7 | G ||
LIT-TLE | STAR | HOW I | WON-DER | WHAT YOU | ARE ||

THE ALPHABET SONG

2/4

G | G | C | G | C | G |
A, B, | C, D, | E, F, | G | H, I, | J, K, |

D7 | G | G | D7 | G | D7 |
L, M, N O | P, | Q, R, | S, and | T, U, | V, |

G | D7 | G | D7 | G | G |
W double | you and | X, Y, | Z, | HAP-PY | HAP-PY

C | G | C | G | D7 | G ||
SHALL WE | BE. | WHEN WE | LEARN OUR | A, B, | C ||

I hope you enjoy the new song Darlings. There is nothing worse than reaching a snag, and being left in a lurch. It could be very frustrating when this happens. I am sure you have sailed through so far. It makes me happy to see you happy. Let us continue this song, with the same results.

WABASH CANNON BALL

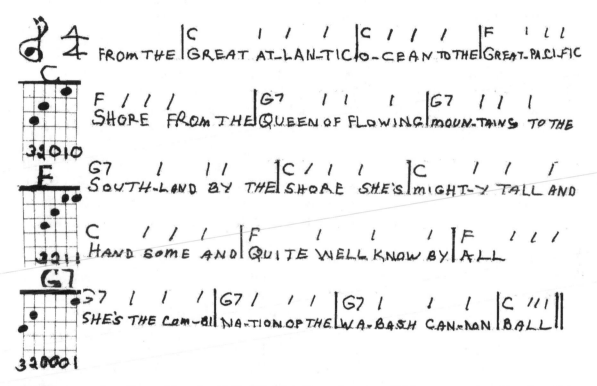

This song has three Chords. C-F-G7. The C we know. G7 is a new one. To play this Chord, drop the hand down and bring it up slowly. When you go out for a walk, stop and bring your arm up half way, and look at it. It is always in its natural position. The hand is not straight out, nor is it in a fist. In playing the Piano or Guitar, or anything like walking or whatever it is in its natural position Dears.

The G7 Chord is played thus: Turn the palm toward you. The 1st finger on the 1st string of the 1st fret becomes F. The next three strings are open B G D. The fifth string on the 2nd fret and 2nd finger becomes B. The sixth string on the 3rd fret with the 3rd finger becomes G. Lastly, the F Chord is somewhat difficult, as two strings must be played at the same time with the same finger. To better accomplice this is to turn the arm toward the waist.

21

The 1st finger will play the 1st fret of the 1st string, and also the second string of the 1st fret with the same finger Dears. I hope this does not cause you much distress, but that is what it is. This will give us F and C. The 2nd finger will play the second fret on the 3rd string A. The 4th string is used with the 3rd finger on the 3rd fret. This will give us F. Only four strings are played.

The "Wabash Cannon Ball" starts with an incomplete measure. On measure 16 you will find the rest of the measure. It was split because of the verse. We have two measures of C Chords, two of the F Chords, three of the G7 Chords, three more of the C, two of the F chords, and three more of the G7, and end on the C.

Take the time to compare the Piano Version (Page 11) with the Guitar Version. I am sure if you had never studied Piano, the guitar version would look like two different worlds. Most Guitarists are well vested in Chords. Build entire careers on just this segment. This is only a section of the whole. Life being as wonderful as it is, to be able to carve out a living on pure Chords is miraculous.

Playing in most Bands that is all that is required, but at times a Riff is added (a melodic phrase repeated again and again). This adds interest to the music. Of course Pianists play Chords, but not to the extent as a Rock and Roller. Chords are a must in this department, as the vocalist or another instrument takes up the melody.

Looking at Popular Piano Music Version of the hits of the day, notice they also have the Chords written out. In modern music of this sort we don't have to have the Bass exposed. All we have to do is play Chords with the left hand, and the melody with the right hand. If we don't know our Chords, however, we could be in for a rough ride.

We will combine this subject in the next Chapter on Piano. For this demonstration we go to Chapter Four, (Page 23) Darlings, and charge ahead. We will take up another piece, but it will be in the Key of G. Best to stay in something familiar if the piece is new. This one is a Spiritual Song, "Go Tell It On The Mountain".

We could accompany any melody, and make it appear "full bodied". It is a grand way to perform a piece of music, without actually reading the Bass Notes of a Piano Piece. For this I will show a Piano Chart, and you will discover they are the same Chords that are played on the Guitar.

This is one way of enforcing on the mind how to utilize and put to use something that already has been studied. Some people who play by ear (never studied, but can play to some degree, having good pitch) can cut up a storm, and get noticed, but don't understand what is happening. So Dears, enough chitchat and lets get started.

****

CHAPTER FOUR

*****

LESSON 4

MELODY WITH CHORDS

The same Chords we use for the Guitar, we also utilize for the Piano. They are one and the same. The only difference is that they adapt to the instrument in use. In Piano the Bass Notes are quite difficult to grasp at the beginning, but improve with time. The Chart shows the Bass Clef Sign on the fourth line, meaning that the note F will always appear on this fourth line, and all the others will read from there.

On the Piano the Chords are in plain view, all written out and easy on the eyes. The Guitar, being a different instrument, has the Chords placed above the Melody. All that you see are the letters of the alphabet. **A-B-C-D-E-F-G**. So, when the player has (for instance) the letter **A** placed above the music, it means the **A Chord** is played. One might wonder: What is this **A Chord**. What does it consist of?

It looks like an invisible Chord. If a person has never studied music this will seem like that is the end of it. In the mind it is recognized as a Chord, and to some that is the end of the story. Nothing comes after that. But again Chords are derived from a source, and of all places (the scales). This is the place of origin.

So, like it or not, this is where all the kernel of information is kept. From this we build the mountain of music in the world. It is like planting a seed in the ground, and all things grow from it. What can I say! The scales are really magical, I would say having extraordinary powers. I believe they are not appreciated enough.

We should devote more time to them, and look with new earnest vigor to add strength to our music endeavor, in an attempt to accomplish this mission Dears.

THE GRAND STAFF

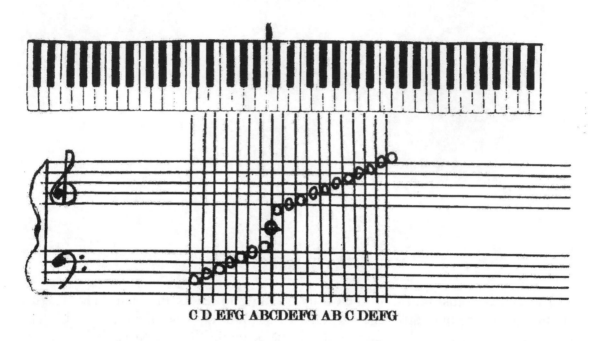

C D EFG ABCDEFG AB C DEFG

SCALE IN CONTRARY MOTION

I won't analyze at this time what you see Dears. You could look at it and see if you could figure it out. Some who have studied the piano might know what the Grand Staff is, but the Guitars players who have never come across it will have a problem. For now we will start our new piece.

GO TELL IT ON THE MOUNTAIN

The first measure is a half note and gets two beats. The next four notes are dotted eighths and sixteenth notes. How to play them? Well, start from the beginning of the first measure. Rest your arm as we did before, and count. Drop the foot and the index finger on the count of **ONE**, it helps to use the foot at times, hold the **AND**, plus the **TWO**, bring it up silently on **AND**.

Tap the **foot** with the **finger** on the **third** beat, the foot and the finger come down at the same time on this beat, bring the **foot** plus **finger** up silently, (the dotted 8th note is the **AND**) then snap both finger and foot (down and up rapidly) after you say the AND to play the **sixteenth** note. Since you are up, come down on the count of **4** and repeat the procedure.

The third measure, Finger and foot play the **1st beat**. Come up with only the finger (you can't play with the finger up) snap the finger down and play on the count of **AND**. The Foot plays the count of **TWO**, (finger pops up at this time). Finger should be up at this point. Then the finger snaps down to play the **AND**. Finger is up at this point, snap down and up, for the **3rd beat** hold the **AND**, finish with the **4th beat** hold the **AND**. Dears don't try this if you are not up to it. Wait until you are really ready then give it a try.

THE GUITAR VERSION

Now the Guitar Version is much easier. One does not have to read music. All we need at this point are three chords. How simple is that? The Chords are G-D7-and A7. Stripping it down to its bare bones to further simplify the subject, we need not to know or ponder over the 7 next to the name of the Chord. This is of no consequence if we so desire it not to be. We could still play the Chords, as the book we have before us at the moment have the Chords written out.

The problem with this picture is that the student may be only interested in a fast route to start playing without much effort. Reaching this stage gives the mind not much to do, so the interest is not strong enough to go ahead. The mind needs more stimulation to spur and latch on to something concrete.

Otherwise, we fall short going upwards without attaching to a purpose. When a subject becomes frivolous it is of little value. Best to spend time and absorb as much as possible to reach the next stage. So the motto of the story is: the brain has preference or the power over our desires.

When you are watching T.V. and are about to black out: have your music near you. It is truly amazing how the brain picks up on this and is happy to finally get attention. This is very true! When one is outdoors, no matter how long, it seems all is well. But do you notice when you arrive home, the body changes. It knows you are HOME; it is a little scary at times because it knows too much, and one becomes a different person, for the better of course.

D SCALE CHART

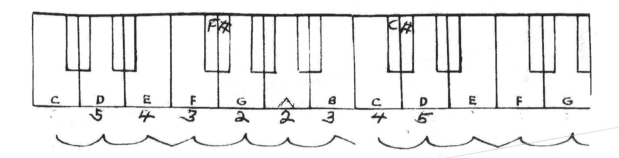

The pattern for the D SCALE is written out. Notice it is the same as the C and the G SCALE. The new SCALE D follows the same rule. One more # has been added to the one existing #. The new sharp is C#. What is amazing if you look carefully is that these #'s go up in 5th's. So far we have Two Sharps. Lets count them. The first one was F#, counting 5 up from this Sharp gave us C#.

This exact design is complete in all respect. I believe you can't help but feel happy when you accomplish this mission. We now have three scales we could call our own. C-G-D. It is not something you have memorized and can easily forget. When there is knowledge behind this, it is there to stay.

While we are on the D SCALE we will extract a D CHORD from it. This will hold true with all of the MAJOR SCALES.

PATTERN FOR MAJOR CHORDS

Starting on the SCALE OF D MAJOR we need TWO WHOLE STEPS from D. and then a STEP and ONE HALF. Since we have the D SCALE CHART in front of us it will make it clear. Look at the SCALE, starting from D, count the two steps. D to F# make two whole steps. F# to A is one and a half step. D-F# A is a D CHORD.

So knowing the SCALES do make a difference. They not only house the hundreds of CHORDS there are use, but like the seeds in the ground, give us our daily food supplies. Think of NATURE, (the sum total of all things in time and space). Need I say more?

GUITAR GRID CHORDS

When you buy a Guitar book you see the names of the 6 strings of the instrument and Grids with the names of the Chords above it. In each Grid are circles to indicate where to press the finger down to play the Chord. Now a Guitarist who has never studied the Piano, or had Theory Lessons, thinks there in nothing beyond that. But there is life out yonder. It is like opening a door to a new world.

When that door is opened, and the discovery of those Chords are found to have come from "THE SCALES"; this is something new. These so called "Hidden Chords" are finally exposed out in the open. So, when you see (for instance) a C Major Chord in its full glory, having been born from the Scale, it may seem strange at first. It is good to know it does exist, aside from the Grid Form.

We now have some samples of these Chords. The best way to bring them out in the open is from some Piano Music. So, Darlings I will get them out of my Music Cabinet, and show some of them to you. Well, I went through a ton of them, and came up with this Folk Song: "Careless Love".

We only have three Chords: D-G-A. The D Chord consists of D-F# A. The G Chord is G-B-D, and the A Chord is A-C#-E. If you look carefully, it will make clear that these 3 Chords, built on the D Scale, have all of the notes found in the Key of D. These are called the Primary Chords. In other words I is the 1st note of the Scale. The IV is the 4th note, and V is the 5th note of the Scale. The Chord is a combination of three or more tones sounded together in harmony.

The melody is played with the right hand, and the Bass Clef Chords are played with the left hand. The 1st measure (Page 29) has four D Chords. The fingering for the Chords is, starting from the bottom 5-3-1. We use the same fingering for all of the Chords in the piece.

3 CHORDS IN THE KEY OF D

D CHORD   G CHORD   A CHORD

CARELESS LOVE

MELODY AND CHORD VERSION

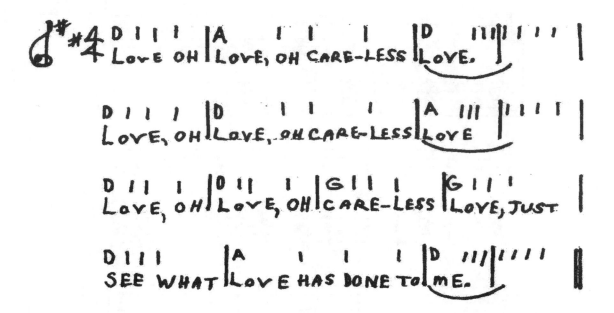

MELODY

3 VERSIONS OF CARELESS LOVE

A Piano Version---A Chord Version--- and one with a melody. Instead of strumming just Chords on the Guitar, try playing the Melody, and combine the Chords with them.

We will go over the Piano Version (Page 29) at this time. In measure 10, notice the A Sharp placed in front of the note. There is no A Sharp in the Key Signature, so this

Sharp is an accidental. The rules are that the composer is not iron bound in this respect. As he goes along composing, and needs some of these accidentals along on the musical journey, he has the liberty and freedom to use them. This also can be erased, if so desired, by using a cancel sign.

Measures 3 and 4, 7 and 8, plus 15 and 16 are all tied notes. This means that the melody note is held for the two measures, and played only one time, but the Chords continue as an accompaniment to the music. As you notice, the Piano version looks different from the other two. The actual Chords have not changed, only the instrument has.

Familiarize yourself with all three types, and analyze other music of the same type. So, Dears, you have plenty of work cut out for you. Go slowly, but thoroughly digest to make sure you understand what has transpired. Take notice that the two Guitar Versions have everything intact, as so does the Piano one. They just look different.

Music requires much mental concentration. I recall when I was going to a Music School in New York City, one woman student, wife of a Doctor, was very agitated as we were going down the stairs. She said, "I couldn't understand a thing in that Theory Class." I explained to her in plain English what she was concerned about. Her face lit up and she said with great relief, "I understand you perfectly."

If knowledge is imparted in such a way that it is easily understood, life is much better for it. Many people are left on the wayside for the very reason that it is not very well understood. Well, lets face it: Not everyone happens to be in the right career. If the ability to impart information is lacking, pity the poor student. However, all is not lost, as the serious student will find the way eventually.

In our next piece: "Shenandoah" (Page 32) The Piano Version Bass Chords has half notes. We play only 2 Chords per measure, instead of the 4 in the previous song. This is for diversification. It starts with the weak beat: Oh, and the strong beat is Shenandoah. We will play with the index finger, and also use our foot. If you are in public, use your toes to get the same results.

The hands could be clasped together, and the finger could do the counting under the palm of the hand. We can't ask for more privacy Dears. The finger presses the palm on the count of FOUR AND, release the pressure on the AND. The next measure: press the fingers and the toes at the same time on the count of ONE. Both come up, but only the finger plays the AND, and lands on the count of TWO AND, but this AND comes up silently. The 3rd beat only the FOOT plays on the count of THREE, the AND played by the finger, and continues to play the finger on the count of FOUR with the AND played.

If you find this to tedious Dears, skip it for now, or to please me continue, as we have a few more rough spots. The 2nd measure looks rather fearful so lets clear it up.

SHENANDOAH

Both FOOT with FINGER come down on the count of ONE with the AND up silently, landing on the count of TWO AND. Since this does need much fixed attention Dears, try each beat alone, until absorbed. We then go to the 2nd beat and so forth, until all of the 4 beats are completed. We better go over the second measure, as that looks rather foreboding. The first beat ONE, the FOOT with the FINGER, come down together, the finger comes up on the AND, but is silent. Only the FINGER comes down on the count of TWO AND, while that is being held, the FOOT plays the count of THREE. While that is being held, the FINGER pops up on the AND to play the FOUR AND.

I hope I didn't tax you too much, Dears. I think I will let you figure the rest out for yourself, because I'm getting tired. The two Guitar Versions I will also leave up to you. Sorry Dears for giving you the job, but we must share in the task.

GUITAR VERSIONS OF SHENANDOAH

CHORD VERSION

CHAPTER FIVE

*****

LESSON 5

PIANO AND GUITAR CHART

So far we have had the **C-G and D SCALE.** If we count 5 up from the **D SCALE** we reach the next one, which is the **A SCALE. The A SCALE has 3 #'s.** If we review, and recall, the C did not have any. G had only 1#. D went up to 2#'s Now the A picked up a 3rd #. This system is flawless. Count 5 from the A SCALE and we get the E SCALE, and of course we pick up another #, which gives us 4 #'s. Below are the 2 added SCALES.

A---E---SCALE

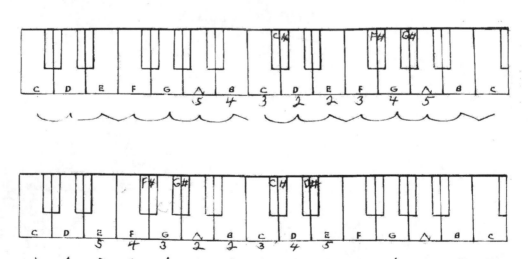

GUITAR CHART

E	A	D	G	B	E	
F	A#	D#	G#	C	F	1
F#	B	E	A	C#	F#	2
G	C	F	A#	D	G	3
G#	C#	F#	B	D#	G#	4
A	D	G	C	E	A	

This Chart shows the 6 Guitar Strings, and the Frets that house them. The First Position on the Guitar has the fingering thus: 1-2-3-4. The rest of the strings all have the same fingering. The first string is called open E. When the left hand presses the 1st FRET with the 1st finger down on this string, the open E becomes a new note, which is called F. So, Dears, what is happening is that this process continues, and we have new notes being born all over the place.

The 2nd finger presses the next FRET, and we have F#. The 3rd finger presses the next FRET, and we have the note G, and lastly, the 4th finger presses the next FRET, and we have a G#. The other 5 strings follow the same pattern. Isn't it wonderful how it all falls into this arrangement. It certainly seems that LIFE is very orderly, and lets face it, this did not happen by chance.

HAND POSITION

To play the strings, we could use a PICK, to peck at it, which is about the only thing to use on the ELECTRIC GUITAR, as we are playing STEEL STRINGS. If a CLASSICAL GUITAR is used, being with NYLON STRINGS, we normally use our fingers. For this bit of exercise, the right hand prepares the process by using the 1st finger.

At the beginning of a Work Book the student is required to learn the 1st string by playing the open E, then the F and G note. The 2nd string follows the same route: playing the open B string, and the C and D. This continues until all 6 strings have a smithereens or only a small fragment of broken pieces. That is all well and done, but I decided to lay- out the whole 1st position at the beginning to show what lies between this mysterious set up. (The 1st position means that the 1st finger of the left hand is placed on the 1st fret, 2nd finger on the 2nd fret and so on to the 3rd and 4th Fret.)

In other words an advance look at what is coming. We do go into the beginners mode, but at least we know where we are going, and why this was constructed in this manner. Who wants to be kept in the dark? Since we have some Knowledge of Scales, it makes more sense to open up this dialogue. Keep the Guitar Chart handy, until memorized.

Darlings we are still dealing with only the 1st seven letters of the Alphabet. A-B-C-D-E-F-G. As we journey along, and things get complicated, it is easy to forget how we got started. So Dears keep in mind that the half step is between B and C, and E and F. After that the traveling goes as high as the moon. To keep from getting lost, each step must be assimilated as thoroughly as possible. This is one reason why pupils disappear in mass numbers.

Once you understand the Guitar Chart it will dawn on you that the reason all those Guitar Books, and I will do it also for clarification, was for its simplicity. Take a gander on how these particular notes were chosen. Look carefully and you will see they are surrounded, and overwhelmed by the complicated #'s. How could they be explained except for the Knowledge of the SCALES, and how they began life.

Darlings, spending time on a worthwhile endeavor, is like saving for a rainy day. It gives comfort to the soul. It also gives solace and an easing of grief, and loneliness. It is never too late to start: either to pick it up again, or to begin fresh. Music is not like a regular job, as for earning a living. After that has run its course, and retirement occurs, with a sigh of relief: What is left for some is an empty feeling.

With music this does not occur, because music is ethereal. I am not talking about noisy discordant, disagreeable sounds. That is not music. Real music brings one to a higher level. Shall we name one Composer? We all have our very own that is with us. It is unearthly, so out of this world that Life is worth living in it.

FINDING MUSICAL NOTES ON THE GUITAR

SECOND STRING

THIRD STRING

THE FOX

CRAWDAD SONG

COCKLES AND MUSSELS

Well Dears, we had quite a separation from each other. All that hard work learning the 1st three strings: Then 3 new songs using only these 3 strings. Best way to learn something new is to fix it firmly into the mind by actually combining the two aspects. Taking each string: not rushing through, and causing confusion, is the right way to reach the desired goal.

In the 3rd measure of THE FOX: the counting is: FOOT with INDEX finger go down on the count of ONE, the AND goes up being silent (the foot also comes up). Second beat the FOOT and FINGER come down on the TWO, this time plays the AND, then both pop up, and lands on the next beat. The FOOT and the INDEX finger come down on the THREE, with the AND being held (only the FOOT comes up). Then only the FOOT comes down on the FOUR at the same time the finger pops up, and play the AND. Measure 14 has a tied note, meaning do not play the measure 15 again, only hold for the full count.

That was quite a workout Dears. If you go to a GYM it is no different. A workout is just that, except this one is for the BRAIN. Many Music Conductors learn their whole orchestra scores away from the instruments. Some who were sickly, and had to spend time in bed, did their mental work while recuperating. I recall when I had to play in recitals: I would go over my pieces in my mind while waiting for a bus in New York City on some cold snowing days, I kept my mind busy for the coming concert.

Most students playing in public become nervous wrecks, and usually play badly because of it. The insecurity is caused by lack of memorization. The habit of some to rely on total finger power is a mistake. A piece that is embedded in the mind will burst forth effortlessly.

I remember one student was so nervous when she came on stage; she stood in front of the Piano as though she was afraid to sit down. Then she calmly took off her ring and put it on the Piano and sat down. Suddenly she plowed into her Beethoven Sonata, which lasted less than a minute, and stopped! She looked at the audience, as though it was their fault. Then she started over again, and finished without incident.

Another picture comes to mind. This was a teenage boy. He sat down, put his fingers on the keyboard of the Grand Piano, and nothing came out. His fingers froze on the piano, and he couldn't move them. He had to get up and leave the stage. All this comes from not having the music firmly entrenched in the mind.

It is true when a student says, " I can't remember a note." This is because the piece was memorized by finger power only. If there is nothing in the brain, then the statement is true. This will cause great stress.

Of course, using the brain is difficult. But like everything else, with practice all will be well. Each person has his own way of doing things. In some the interest is extremely strong, and nothing will deter if a set back happens. So keep at it Dears.

CHAPTER SIX

*****

LESSON 6

MORE ON THE GRAND STAFF

Looking at the GRAND STAFF (page 24), notice that the Middle C is in the center of the Treble and Bass staff. Take the Middle C and count upwards. C-D-E-F-G-A-B-C-D-E-F-G. It does go higher of course, but we will go only up to the high G. Now for the difficult part: Go back to the same Middle C and count backwards Dears.

Middle C going down: C-B-A-G-F-E-D-C-. Do you notice something strange? Look at the High G in the Treble Staff, and the High G in the Bass Staff. They look the same, but one reads G, and the other reads B. How did that happen? Well, the Treble and the Bass read differently.

When you come down from the high G (treble) the next note coming down is F. But, from the Bass note that seems to read like the same G, we get a B. This is the dividing point. So, Dears let us confront this matter. You will notice that this High G in the Treble is a Major Third from the Bass B. Do keep in mind that a Major Third is derived from Two Whole Steps.

The Note next to the B in the Bass is A. Think about this: If G (Treble) and Bass B is a Third, and then the next Notes are F and A, another Third something must be going on. Indeed it is! Check all the other Notes, in this fashion, and you will notice that they are all Thirds from each other. This is done very orderly in a proper sequence.

This also works coming down Starting from the Bass B, and the Treble G. Continuing from the A and F and so forth. So it works both ways UP or DOWN. The Third as you recall comes from the Scales, where else. When you see a Bass Note that looks like an A, flip your thinking, and turn it into a Third, and immediately you get C. When you see an E, do the same thing. Think a Third ahead, and turn it into a G. Keep the practice Darlings, and you will be in good hands.

SAMPLE OF LITTLE BROWN JUG

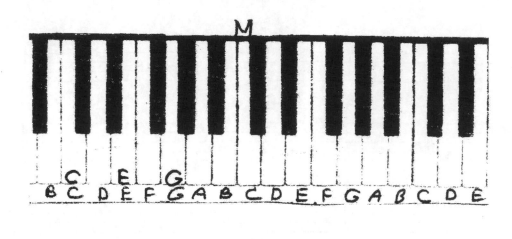

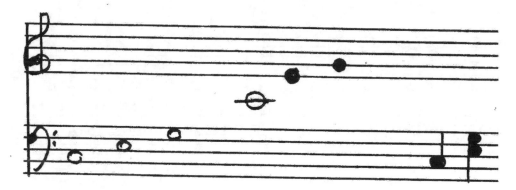

The Piano Keyboard shows where the Chords are located in the next piece. As you see from Middle C the Bass is one Octave lower than the C. Count 8 Keys from C to C. When you see two double notes clumped together that is only part of a Chord. A triad is a
Musical Chord of three tones especially one consisting of a Root Tone and its 3rd and 5th. The triad gets it name from the Root. For instance the Root of a C triad is C. The Chord is a combination of three or more tones sounded together in harmony.

THE PRIMARY TRIADS

In any key the 3 most important triads are the ones built on the 1st, 4th, and 5th notes of the scale. We use Roman Numerals thus: 1,1V, and V. for the (1st, 4th and 5th) So Dears in the Key of C, the 1 Chord is the C Triad- The 1V Chord is the F Triad, and the V Chord if the G Triad. This all comes from the Scales,

46

LITTLE BROWN JUG

47

THE OLD CHISHOLM TRAIL

SKIP TO MY LOU

Skip To my you my dar - ling.

D.C.

Dears, I did not forget you in explaining "The Old Chisholm Trail" (Page 48). We are in the Key of D. The Piano Version has 2 different Chords in one measure. This pattern runs throughout the whole song. Notice that some of the notes look different from the other pieces. This has to do with the Verse. If there are many Verses, then the words have to fit the music. One set will go well with it, but another one will have more words.

Starting from the first measure, we will identify a quarter note by virtue of the stem going up on the right hand side. The lower stem attached to it is on the left side, happens to be an eighth note. Next to it is another eighth note. Remember this is for the verse to fit the words if we happen to have that situation.

2nd Verse
I start-ed up the trail- on a cold and cloudy day--I –
Start-ed up the trail-with the lone Star- herd.-
CHORUS
Com-a ti yi yip-py, yip-py yay, yip-py yay, Com-a
Ti yi yip-py yip py yay.___I

The end of the 2nd Verse with the-I- means to start with the 3rd Verse at the beginning of the Piece. If you feel so inclined, you could make up your own Verse. Just make sure that you fit the music. This is an old Cowboy Song.

SKIP TO MY LOU

I will put another Song with the same outline as the "Old Chisholm Trail" to better understand the process.(Page 49) We are in the Key of G. The 1st measure starts out with a quarter note. The 2nd beat has a quarter note with the stem going down on the left side and the eighth note attached to it on the right side. Another eighth without any fill in of verse, perhaps waiting for another word from a 2nd go around. The 3rd beat has a quarter note with the stem going up on the right side. The attached eighth onto the left side, and the 4th beat is a repeat.

The end of the piece has a D.C.: stands for from the beginning. It is a repeat sign, and is ready for the 2nd Verse.

2nd Verse
I lost my girl-Now- what-will I do?
I lost my girl-Now-what-will I do?
I lost my girl-Now-what will I do?

CHORUS
Skip To My Lou My Dar - ling.

CHAPTER SEVEN

*****

LESSON 7

RETURNING TO THE GUITAR

Darlings, we did the first three strings. This was the First, Second, and the Third Strings. Doesn't it feel great to return to something that was left behind? We know part of it was worked on so it does not seem a total stranger to us. It does show that whatever we do there is a record of it. When you think about it: that whatever ground has been covered, it has made its mark.

On page 40, the piece called the "The Fox" had the Notes of the First Two Strings. The 1st string which consisted of Open E, and the 1st Fret of F and the 3rd Fret of G. We used only two notes on the 2nd string, and that was a C, found on the 1st Fret, and the D on the 3rd Fret. So the whole Song was played on the Guitar using only the two strings of 5 Notes.

The "Crawdad Song" on page 41, used the 1st three strings. The open E string, the 2nd string with an open B, and the D on the 3rd Fret of this same string. The 3rd string of G was used with the open G, and the A on the 2nd Fret. Total notes were 5.

The "Cockles and Mussels" on page 42 used the 1st open E string, and the F on the 1st Fret, and also the high G on the 3rd Fret. The 2nd string was the 1st Fret C, the 3rd Fret D. The 3rd string open G. Total notes were 6. Now we will start learning the next three strings, which will be a total of the 6 Guitar Strings.

The next in order is the open 4th string, called D. Then E found on the 2nd Fret, and F on the 3rd Fret. The 5th string is open A. On this string is B on the 2nd Fret, and C on the 3rd Fret. Finally we are on the last string called open E. The F is on the 1st Fret and G on the 3rd Fret. Notice that the High E (1st string) and the Low E (6th string) are the same, except for the sound.

FOURTH STRING

52

FIFTH STRING

53

REVIEW OF THE LAST THREE STRINGS

Take notice that the 4th string of Open D, is an Octave lower than the D we had on the second string of the third Fret.

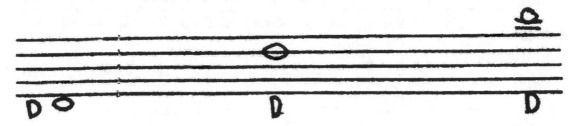

The 5th string of Open A is an Octave lower than the A found on the third string of the second Fret.

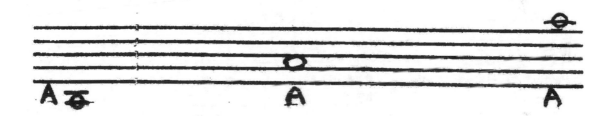

The 6th string of Open E is two Octaves lower than the E found on the first string of Open E. However, there is another E on the 4th string of the second Fret.

We will find a song that incorporates the first four strings. This is the E-B-G-and D. I am sure this will cement in the mind the memory of these strings. So Dears let us get started on this all-important mission. The Song I chose is: "The Foggy, Foggy Dew" It is in the Key of G, and starts with the open D note on the 4th string. It ends on the G note on the open 3rd G-string. There is nothing really new, so I trust you to play well, and enjoy the accomplishment you have gained so far.

THE FOGGY, FOGGY DEW

CHORDS FOR THE SONGS

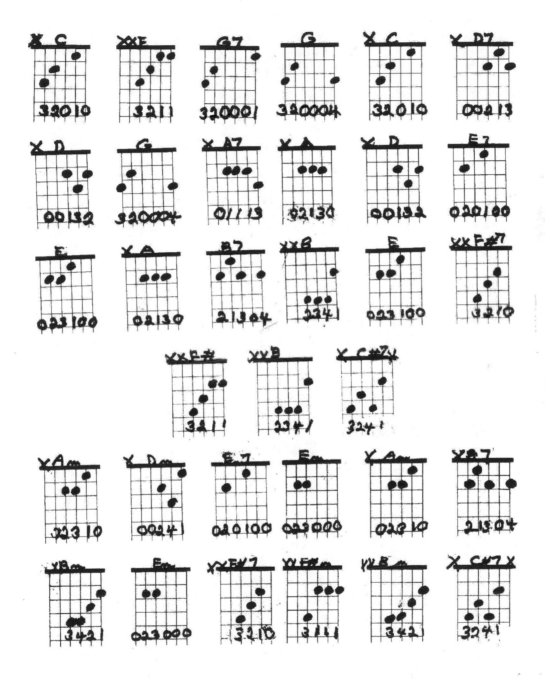

ADDED CHORDS

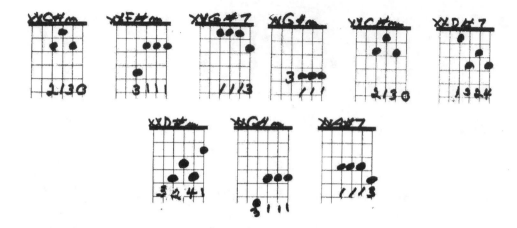

The most important Chords in any Key are the 3 Primary Chords. They are built on the 1st, 4th and the 5th notes of the scale. The reason I put the Chords in sets of three was to demonstrate that these three Chords can be harmonized with any melody. For instance: the first set is in the Key of C, the 3 Primary chords are C-F-G7 Along side of it is the 2nd set G-C-D7, and so on until we reach the 7th set.

Dears, the next sets are the Minor Chords. I am only introducing the minor at this time just so you can get familiar that they are alive and well. I really don't think you may be ready for this, but no harm in letting your know what is lurking ahead. As for now we said that the Minor Chords are derived from the Major Chords. That is true. We begin with the C Chord. The Relative minor of C is A minor. If we count 6 from C we get the A minor Chord.. C-D-E-F-G-A. The 1- 1V- V- of the A minor reads: A-D-E7

Very important to remember: Each of the Major Keys has a Relative Minor Key. They are so called because they share the same Key Signature. If you take the G Scale, and look at the Key Signature, we see F#. The Minor of the G Scale, counting up the 6 tones, we get the E Minor Scale. Even though this is a minor key it shares the same Key Signature as the G Major Scale.

One point of interest: since the minor Chords came from the Relative Major, and they share the same Key Signature they do not share the same scale. This minor Scale is called Harmonic, and the pattern is different from the Major Scale. Not to worry, as this is just a look ahead to let you know the music world has no end. The reality is neither has any other subject. One cannot close the door on anything, as life has a continuing process with an open door.

WHAT A FRIEND WE HAVE IN JESUS

What a Friend we have in Je-sus,
All our sins and griefs to bear!
What a pri-vi-lege to car-ry
Ev-'ry- thing to God in prayer!
O what peace we oft-en -for-feit,
O what need-less pain we bear,
All- be-cause we do not car-ry
Ev-'ry thing to God in prayer.

IT CAME UPON A MIDNIGHT CLEAR

It came up-on a mid-night clear,
That glo-rious song of old,
From an-gels bend-ing near the earth,
To touch their harps of gold.
"Peace on the earth- good will to men,
From heav'n's all gra-cious King."
The world in sol-emn still-ness lay ---
To hear the an- gles sing.

CHAPTER EIGHT

*****

LESSON 8

PIANO AND GUITAR SCALES

Dears, we have come a long journey, so far. We will pick up the threads from the last Scale of E. If you recall we counted five from the last Scale. E-F-G-A-B. The new arrival is B. Now think back on how we figured how many Sharps #'s this new one will have. The Scale of E had 4 #'s. Check this one to see the 4 we left behind. We started with the 1st one, which was F#. Think back again and find the Key it belongs to.

If you forgot this just count 5 from E backwards-E-D-C-B-A and the Key of A had 3 # Continue 5 from A, and we have A-G-F-E-D, and the Key of D has 2 #'s. Count 5 from D, D-C-B-A-G and the Key of G has 1 #.

So if we continue in this fashion, and count 5 upwards from E (where we left off) with the 4 #'s. To find out how many #'s the Scale of B has, it must then have 5#'s. How do we come to that conclusion?

We are going upwards now, so Darlings count 5 from E, and a B occurs. Count 5 from B, and the Key of F# pops up, and we have 6 #'s (Remember it cannot be a plain F, as we already had our 1st # in the Key of G.) So 5 from F# gives us the Key of C#, and we end up for now with 7 #'s.

We will not go into the Flat Keys, as it would be too confusing at this time. There is plenty of time for that at another lesson. The brain could only take so much information, and keep it at a comfortable level. If too much is given at one session it could revolt. As for me I will have a cup of coffee after all that work.

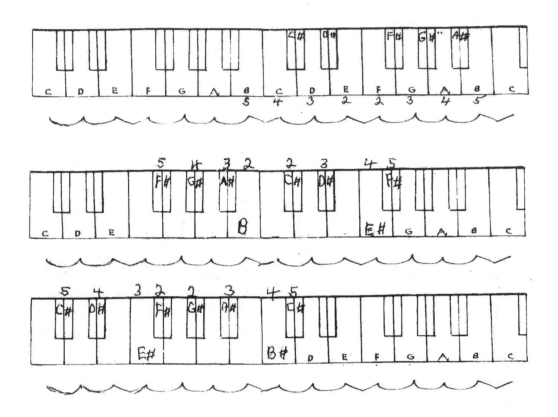

We have the added Scales of B-F# and C#. Take notice that the F# Scale starts on the Black Key, as so the C#. This should be firmly embedded in the mind. The fingering for these last two Keys on the Piano will be thus: The 4th finger of the left hand goes on the F#, and the 2nd finger of the right hand on the F#. The C# Scale the 3rd finger on the C# of the left hand, and the 2nd finger of the right on the C#.

Of course the Guitar uses the same Scales as does all other instruments, including the human voice, which is really another musical instrument. The difference changes drastically only on the instruments used, as for instance: the Guitar. The actual Scales do not change, but they must apply to the 6 strings that we are to play. The foundation of knowing this knowledge is indispensable One could carry misinformation for life; never knowing at what point it got messed up. Moving along in an orderly fashion is the way to go with any learning process.

C SCALE FOR PIANO AND GUITAR

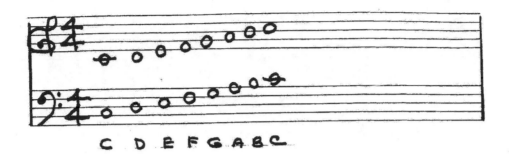

C D E F G A B C

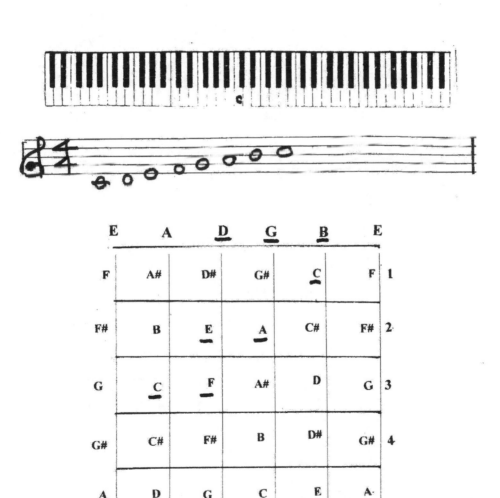

	E	A	D	G	B	E	
1	F	A#	D#	G#	C	F	1
2	F#	B	E	A	C#	F#	2
3	G	C	F	A#	D	G	3
4	G#	C#	F#	B	D#	G#	4
5	A	D	G	C	E	A	

C Scale has no Sharps or Flats. Piano Chart shows the Treble and the Bass Notes. Guitar Chart has the Treble only as the Guitar does not have the Bass. Below you will find the G Scale written out on the Chart. Good luck Dears.

G SCALE FOR PIANO AND GUITAR

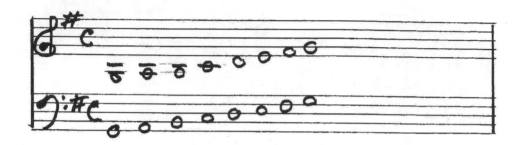

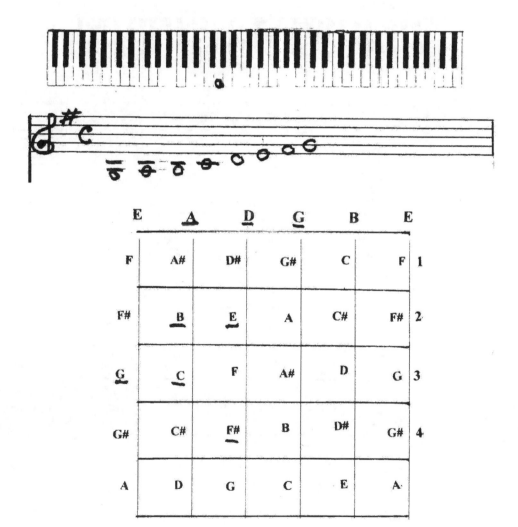

G Scale has one # - (F Sharp)

D SCALE FOR PIANO AND GUITAR

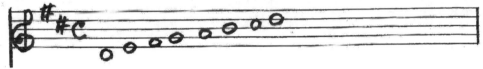

E	A	D	G	B	E	
F	A#	D#	G#	C	F	1
F#	B	E	A	C#	F#	2
G	C	F	A#	D	G	3
G#	C#	F#	B	D#	G#	4
A	D	G	C	E	A	

D Scale has two #'s – (F# - C# Sharp)

65

A SCALE FOR PIANO AND GUITAR

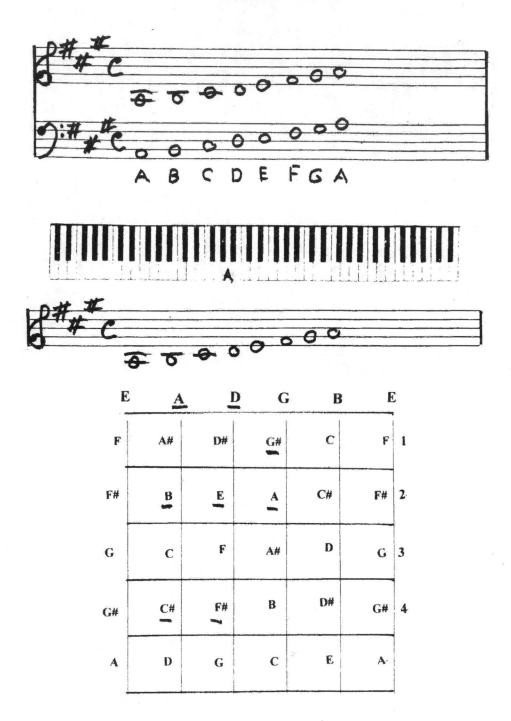

A Scale has three #'s – (F# - C# - G#)

E SCALE FOR PIANO AND GUITAR

E F G A B C D E

E	A	D	G	B	E	
F	A#	D#	G#	C	F	1
F#	B	E	A	C#	F#	2
G	C	F	A#	D	G	3
G#	C#	F#	B	D#	G#	4
A	D	G	C	E	A	

E Scale has four #'s. (F# – C# – G# – D#)

B SCALE FOR PIANO AND GUITAR

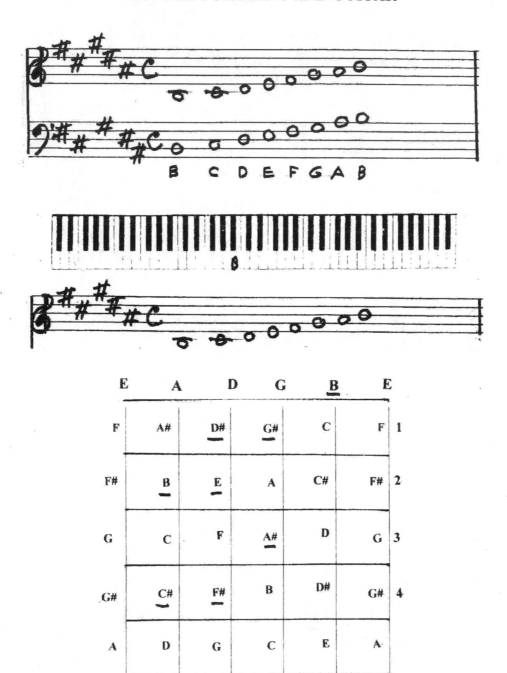

B Scale has five #'s: (F# - C# - G# - D# - A#)

F# SCALE FOR PIANO AND GUITAR

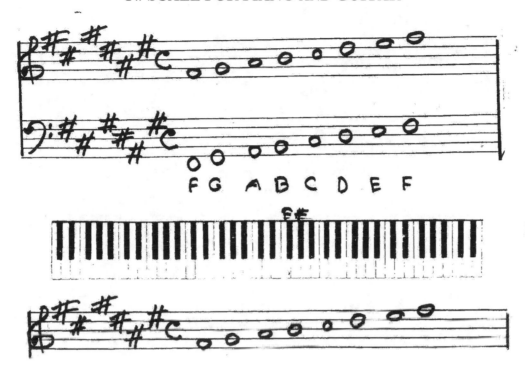

F# Scale has six #'s: (F# - C# - G# - D# - A# - E#)

ATTENTION

E# and F land on the same Key. This is called "Enharmonic Change"

C# SCALE FOR PIANO AND GUITAR

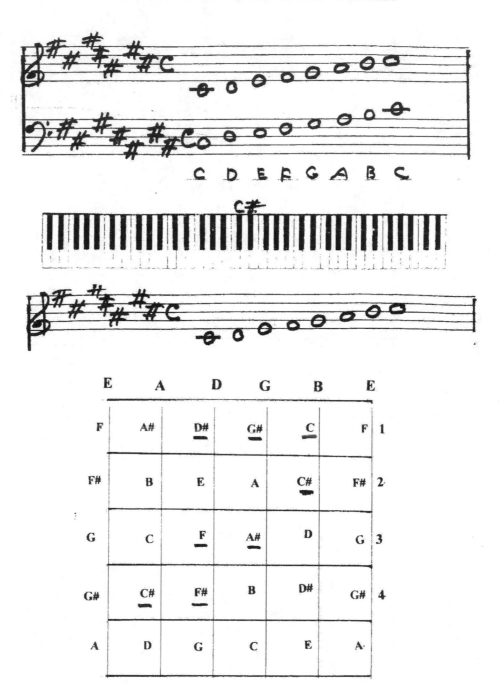

C# Scale has seven Sharps: (F# - C# - G# - D# - A# - E# - B#)
ATTENTION
B# and C also share the same KEY. "Enharmonic Change"

CHAPTER NINE

*****

LESSON 9

REUBEN AND RACHEL (TRANSPOSE)

Well, Darlings, What do you think? Can you handle all the work cut out for you? Music takes time to be absorbed. Have you ever gone to a Major Opera House? The preparation for this colossal performance is breath taking. The effort and perseverance of carrying out such a purpose, and conquering all the obstacles is an experience to behold. In plain English (it is not easy) it takes a lifetime of hard work. What keeps a musician going is the special spark that never dries up.

What to do with all this information? Well we could start right in with a simple Southern Tune called:

"REUBEN AND RACHEL"

It starts in the Key of C. Rachel makes a statement, and then Reuben replies to it. The piece has only eight measures. It stays within the Octave. The end of the music has a repeat sign. We will play this tune in the other 7 Keys. This is transposing: In other words to play a composition in different Keys.

If played on the Guitar we strum just two Chords. The melody has 5 assorted notes. Played on the Piano all we do is add the Bass to the music. To transpose to the next Key, count 5 up from C, and we are in the G mode.

Now Reuben and Rachel are in the Key of G. This is the same tune, but in another Key. If you have never studied music it would be very difficult to understand how they could be connected. We will also play the same song in the Key of D- A- E- B- F#- C#- I picked this tune because it is unembellished with complications, and thus makes it easier to concentrate where it counts. So Dears, I know there are tons of people out in this world who have exceptional brain power, and who could breeze through this, including you as being one of them.

TRANSPOSE IN C

The Key of C has no Sharps or Flats. The 2nd measure has a different note, after the 5 C's. Count 6 up from C and A appears. Since the next note is coming down from A, we could count from C again and reach the G by counting 5 up. Another way is to observe the G and to see it is definitely coming down. The E is only a 3rd up from middle C.. Then we are back to the starting point of C.

Since a Scale consists of 8 tones, and the piece is confined in these 8 notes, we could use another method. This time we will count the numbers. Jot down the C Scale, and number the notes thus: 1-2-3-4-5-6-7-8. Count the 1st C as number 1- then the 2nd C as 1- and so forth .So lets start Dears: 1-1-1-1---1-6-5-3 "Which is Reu-ben Reu-ben--- I've been thin-king." Continue in this fashion:---1-1-1-1---1-6-5—"Life is some-times--- aw-fly queer" 8-8-7-5---6-6-5-3- "No one knows where--- we are going." 1-2-3-1---6-7-8. No one knows why--- we are here-"

When we look at the next Key in order, what do we see? It certainly looks far different from the C version. Without having any "Knowledge of Music" how can a person untangle the mystery of it all! Study them side by side, and without using the information supplied, try to figure it out.

Going to weekly music lessons will not uncover the inner core of the problem. Usually half hour lessons are the norm. Who has the time or the inclination to enter something that is beyond understanding? Music goes back for centuries. Bits and pieces have been added on as time went by, especially by "Johann Sebastian Bach" (1685-1750).

Bach is the family name of several prominent musicians and composers. About 60 to 70 Bachs are known to have been musicians. Many of them were composers, but few of their works are played today. The exceptions are "Johann Sebastian Bach" and his sons "Johann Christian" and "Carl Philipp Emanuel". Johann Sebastian Bach is considered the greatest genius of Baroque Music.

Of course, other Great Composers, before and after Bach added their genius throughout the Centuries of Music. What is amazing is the additions are not mish-mash. For instance one composer said about Beethoven music every note is in the right place. How can that be possible? It seems a Higher Power is guiding the Earthly Being.

It appears to be true! In other professions, such as **Mathematics**, another subject that certainly is not mish-mash. It has the power to solve some of the deepest puzzles man must face. **Arithmetic** deals with quantities---**Algebra** uses quantities and relations expressed by symbols---**Geometry** involves quantities associated with figures in space, such as length and area, and the relationship between figures and space.

Trigonometry is concerned with the measurement of angles and with the relationships of angles. **Analytic Geometry** applies Algebra to Geometric studies. And **Calculus** works with pairs of associated quantities and the way one quantity changes in relation to the other. Continued on Page 81.

TRANSPOSE IN G

TRANSPOSE IN D

TRANSPOSE IN A

TRANSPOSE IN E

TRANSPOSE IN B

TRANSPOSE IN F#

CHAPTER TEN

*****

LESSON 10

MUSIC AND MATH

The Time Signature in Music is a Fraction. The term of a Fraction shows how many of the specified parts of a unit are taken. Numerator and Denominator are used in Arithmetic and Algebra. Arithmetic furnishes the basis of many other branches of mathematics. It includes four basic operations: addition, subtraction, multiplication, and division. It is one of the most useful and fascinating divisions of human knowledge, and has the power to solve some of the deepest puzzles man must face.

FRACTION TERMS

BAR---is a short line that separates a Numerator from the denominator in a Fraction.

Numerator--- is the number written above the bar in a fraction. The numerator of 2/3 is 2. The Numerator tells us how many parts are taken.

Denominator--- is the number written below the bar in a fraction. The Denominator of 2/3 is 3. The Denominator tells us how many parts a whole has been divided

MUSIC FRACTION

In music we use the Fraction in the Time Signature. This tells us that in ¾ time we have 3 beats to a measure, and every quarter note gets one beat. It also makes it very clear that Music in very precise: "strictly defined." With the knowledge of the importance of knowing that the framework of Music is Mathematical, then one can continue on the right   path. So, Dears, with this Knowledge, forge ahead, and climb upwards as high as you wish, and be part of this ever- lasting essential process of life.

About the Author

MARY SEWALL is a member of the New York State Music Teachers Association
Brooklyn Conservatory of Music "Diploma Graduate"

Charted by the Regents of the University of the State of New York

The Music School of the "Henry Street Settlement " ---Award for Excellence